He Never Came Home

Joe Ardizzone climbs into his car and drives into the pages of history.

**The Early History of Sunland, California
Volume 5**

ML Tiernan

He Never Came Home

www.maryleetiernan.com
Second printing April 1, 2015
10 9 8 7 6 5 4 3 2

ISBN 978-0983067245 (Paperback)

©1999 ©2010 MaryLee Tiernan. All rights reserved. No portion of this product may be photographed, scanned, translated, reproduced, copied, or reduced to any tangible or electronic medium or machine-readable form, without the prior written consent of Mary Lee Tiernan.

Photograph on cover courtesy of the Ardizone family. Quote on cover from *The Grim Reapers*, p. 165.

Contents

Elsie 5

The Ardizzones 9

Mafia Connections 17

Life after Joe 25

Footnotes 30

Bibliography 31

The Early History of Sunland, California series 33

Author's Notes

The researcher, like a detective, examines the evidence to try to determine the real story. Unfortunately for researchers, we cannot re-examine witnesses or revisit scenes because in most cases, they have long since disappeared. So we sort through the conflicting data to find the most reliable and logical explanations. I have done my best to follow the clues and weave as authentic a story as possible.

There are two spellings of the family name used in this narrative: Ardizzone and Ardizone. Joe spelt his name with two z's: Ardizzone. Joe's son Tony later changed the spelling of the family name to Ardizone, with one z. The spelling changes according to the timeframe.

My thanks to the staff at Bolton Hall Museum, Tujunga, California, for their assistance with this project.

Elsie

When Elsie Elizabeth Ellenberg arrived in California with her family in 1912, Sunland was already a small country town. The post office and telephone company connected the community to the world. Children attended school. The Free Methodist and Sunland Baptist churches

Pioneer women often carried rifles for protection against wildlife, especially snakes. Elsie (left) and her sister Frances (right) pose in the open vistas characteristic of early Sunland. Photo courtesy of the Ardizone family.

offered Sunday services. Families gathered for picnics, concerts, parades, and other social activities in the park. Automobiles transported passengers to Glendale in the east and to the train or to San Fernando in the west. Two hotels, the elegant Monte Vista and the smaller Park, offered amenities to travelers and vacationing families.

Although residents may have been proud of the progress of their flourishing community, Elsie may have felt she had taken a step back in time. The automobiles bumped over pitted, dirt roads. The telephone worked only a few hours a day. A private home housed the post office. Grizzly bears still roamed through wooded canyons. Open vistas of mountains and acres of citrus and olive trees greeted her instead of the crowded, busy streets of the world she left behind.

Born in 1898, Elsie spent her childhood in New York City. When Elsie was nine, her mother died. Her father moved the children—Elsie and her younger brother and sister, John and Frances—to the home of their grandparents John and Margaret Ellenberg, German immigrants who lived on the second story above their general store. Her father, also named John, continued working as a jewelry engraver, but kept reading about the golden opportunities in California. Elsie's grandparents threatened never to speak to him again if he took the children out West, but the lure of opportunity outweighed the threat. Despite their protests, John packed up his children and boarded a train for the land of sunshine.

So at age 14, Elsie found herself living in a lean-to while her father built a ranch house for $600. The family erected their temporary shelter some distance from town along a dirt road surrounded by fields of sagebrush.[1] Since her father's job in downtown Los Angeles meant a very long commute in those days, care of her brother and sister, including cooking their meals outside on an open fire, fell to Elsie. For pleasure, she enjoyed horseback riding and hiking the local mountain trails, although she quickly learned to carry a gun as protection against coyotes, snakes, bobcats, and other wildlife.

A year later, Elsie met a neighbor riding on horseback through the fields near her home. The six-foot, 25-year-old Joe (Joseph) Ardizzone[2] obviously made an impression. The handsome Italian spoke little English, and Elsie spoke no Italian, but romance has its own language. They married a year afterward, in 1916.

Elsie Ardizzone in newly planted vineyards.
Photo courtesy of Mrs. Josephine Kemp.

The Ardizzones

The Ardizzones came from Sicily, home of the Mafia. Legend credits the beginning of the Mafia to an incident that occurred in the city of Palermo, on March 30, 1282, while the French governed Sicily. A drunken French sergeant, Pierre Druet, accosted a bride-to-be on her way to the church. Terrified, the girl tore away from the Frenchman, fell, and cracked her skull on the church wall. The grief-stricken bridegroom beat the sergeant, screaming "Morte alla Francia!" ("Death to all the French!")

Other Sicilians picked up his cry as the news spread and changed it slightly to "Morte alla Francia Italia anela!" ("Death to the French is Italy's cry!") In the ensuing uprising, most of the French in Sicily were killed. A secret society formed, aimed at protecting poor or ill-treated Sicilians. The society shortened the cry to M-A-F-I-A for its name.[3]

Even though the Ardizzones already owned property in Los Angeles, they bought land in Sunland in the early 1900s. The terrain and weather closely resembled that of their native Sicily, a suitable place for growing grapes from the cuttings brought from Italy. Their vineyards, just to the north of the Ellenberg property, included a house, although they usually stayed there only during the grape harvest.

When Joe and Elsie married, Elsie's father gave them his house and moved to Los Angles with his two younger children. Through the years, Joe transformed the barren fields surrounding it. Most of the acreage, of course, nourished grapevines. Around the house, he first added driveways and fences; then he planted. Truck after truck from the Armstrong nursery arrived with trees, shrubbery, and flowers.

The Ellenberg home later became the Ardizzone residence. On the left is the lean-to where the family lived while building the house. The site became the location of Mt. Gleason Jr. High School. Photo courtesy of Mrs. J. Kemp.

Lawn replaced sagebrush. The trees blossomed and produced plums, apricots, peaches, figs, pomegranates, and nectarines. Even the buildings multiplied. Joe added a barn, a pool hall, storage sheds, chicken coops, and separate living quarters for workers. The homestead at 749 North Walnut became a successful ranch, and its inhabitants enjoyed an unusual lifestyle for a Sunland family.

Tony and Josephine play in their driveway. Behind them, a few roof tops peek above the sage brush in the far distance. Today that empty land is filled by the homes opposite Mt. Gleason Jr. High School.
Photo courtesy of Mrs. J. Kemp.

In 1930, with the renaming of streets, the address changed to 10949 Mt. Gleason Avenue, the future site of Mt. Gleason Junior High School. The 25-30 acre ranch seemed larger because relatives owned the surrounding property, including a water plant and pumping station which stood on the corner of Hillrose Street and Woodward Avenue. A reservoir full of clean water for irrigation tempted many local kids to sneak in for a swim.

Although a foreman, Gasparone ("Sponnie") Cacciatore, oversaw care of the vineyards and orchards of figs and plums as well as the running of the winery, life on the ranch kept Elsie very busy, especially after the birth of her children: Tony in 1917 and Josephine in 1919. Like most Sunland families, Elsie kept a vegetable garden, canned fruit, and made jelly. On weekends, the kids took advantage of their location on Walnut, the main route into Big Tujunga Canyon. Joe built a fruit stand in front of the house, from which they earned as much as $20 a day selling grapes, figs, and plums to passers-by on their way up the canyon. A large basket of grapes sold for 25 cents.

Sundays, the customary gathering day for Italian families, Elsie made tomato paste for the dinner sauce in a big wash tub with a screen for a strainer. Then, following tradition, the men made the sauce. Since the local Valley Center Market on Michigan Avenue (later Foothill

Boulevard) near Summitrose carried only a limited line of groceries, Joe did the 'big' shopping in downtown L.A. for fresh garlic and cheese, pepperoni, salami, anchovies, and other ingredients. The extended Ardizzone family enjoyed eating and singing or just sitting around the table sharing family news on those noisy Sundays.

And what's a ranch without its quota of animals: cows, goats, horses, an aviary with beautiful birds, and Elsie's three yards of chickens for eggs and meat—and a

Elsie, Tony, and Josephine, like other early Sunlanders, often traveled around town in a horse cart. Because of the rutted dirt roads, the going was bumpy and rather slow. Photo courtesy of the Ardizone family.

little amusement. One of the wooden tanks in the chicken yard, used to store the dregs of wine drained from the winery vats, dripped. The chickens loved to drink from the steady trickle of wine causing them to stagger around the yard afterward, much to the delight of the children.

Hay in the barn provided a breeding ground for cats, who often scratched the kids trying to play with the kittens. In the kennels out back, Joe and Elsie raised German shepherds. They gave many of the dogs away, but always kept a minimum of six to patrol at night between the chain link fence and the house. The shrubbery Joe loved and planted around the house obscured a clear view of the road, so the dogs provided protection against unseen enemies.

Elsie's hard work on the ranch did not prevent her from spending time with her children. She usually drove them the one mile back and forth to Sunland School on Hillrose in her Model T. At noon, she brought hot lunches in a picnic basket, and they would sit in the car under the shade of the trees to eat. Most of the school kids joined in playground games or tramped together down to the wash during lunch. Tony and Josephine did not join their classmates in such activities. Name-calling and nasty remarks about their Italian heritage hurt the children and segregated them somewhat from their classmates.

Although Elsie restricted her driving to town, she loved to drive. Any excuse would do to get in the car, including giving lots of rides. The kids particularly enjoyed excursions up Big Tujunga Canyon. While the adults sat inside the Model T, the kids stood on running boards and hung on. Each time they crossed the river, the water splashed across them, making the trip as much fun as the destination.

The same yard and house pictured on page ten
after Joe finished the landscaping and making other improvements.
Photo courtesy of the Ardizone family.

Mafia Connections

In addition to his role as rancher, by 1926, Joe Ardizzone officially served as treasurer of the Italian Protection League with Jack Dragna[4], president of the League and titular head of the Mafia in California. Most of the week, Joe worked at their offices in downtown Los Angles, but he often traveled to Chicago and New York to see Al Capone and other syndicate bosses. Unlike the early Mafia which formed to protect the poor and the weak, the Mafia had evolved into a criminal underworld. It should be noted that in the early 1900s, few, including the government, believed that the Mafia existed or understood its role in organized crime.

Whatever Joe's role and activities in the Mafia may have been, at home he was a good father and husband who treated his family, friends, and neighbors well. A cigar box full of IOUs attested to his generosity in lending money. He also gave supplies when needed. For example, when the neighboring Silva family experienced a period of financial problems, Joe bought food for the family and hay for the horses. Elsie dressed in the finest clothes, accented with lavish jewels. On his trips back East, he always remembered to send his children postcards and returned home laden with gifts of clothing and toys.

While Elsie had learned Italian very quickly, Joe often helped Tony and Josephine with their homework to perfect his English skills. Ironically, since both parents wanted to practice their second language, Joe insisted the children speak English with him, while Elsie insisted they speak Italian to her. Josephine didn't realize her mother wasn't Italian until she was 14.

Although Joe could be generous and affectionate, his children also knew his sterner side. He imposed strict rules, like not riding too far away from home on their bicycles, or always coming straight home from school. The sternness was a measure of protection, like the guard dogs. He knew, better than anyone, the potential danger his Mafia connections imposed on his children. He did not tolerate any backtalk from his children—or anyone else. No one crossed Joe Ardizzone, "Iron Man" of the Mafia.

When home, Joe hosted parties and entertained judges, senators, governors, and law enforcement officials. These well-dressed, affluent guests often gave ten-dollar gold pieces to Tony and Josephine. Fortunately, Elsie deposited the money in the bank; she would need it later. The family often dined at the home of John Steven McGroarty—

journalist, U.S. Congressman, and Poet Laureate of California, who also lived in town.[5] When McGroarty started his Mission Play about the early history of California, Joe rounded up friends and relatives from L.A. to pack the audience. Joe's support of the arts extended to helping several movie stars, including Rudolph Valentino.

Joe Ardizzone raised dogs to patrol the property at night.
Photo courtesy of Mrs. Josephine Kemp.

Every year the family vacationed for three weeks at Venice Beach, but never by themselves. Joe rented a large two-story 'mansion' and invited as many as 30 friends or relatives to share their vacation. Different groups came each year. The women and children stayed all week; children also enjoyed an extended stay at the ranch. The men came on weekends, when they seized the opportunity to visit the gambling boats moored out in international waters. Other vacations included car trips along terrible roads to San Francisco, Monterey, Carmel, and Ensenada, and boat trips to Catalina, Joe's favorite.

Joe loved gambling on horse and dog races, as did Elsie, who had her own bookie. At the ranch, both adults and kids played card games, especially poker, which Josephine learned to play at age five. When the adults played around the big dining-room table, they used coins instead of chips. The kids happily scrambled under the table to retrieve the coins dropped by enthusiastic players.

During Prohibition, Joe became heavily involved with bootlegging. Since he owned his own winery, he could grow grapes and process and bottle wine himself, although his still up in Big Tujunga Canyon was not actually on Ardizzone property. Secret tunnels under the house offered escape routes, underground passages into the vineyards, and access to three cellars for storing wine. One cellar was under the two-car garage, another under the house, and the largest out back, with a secret trap door in the closet of the foreman's house.

Official policy during Prohibition allowed wineries to continue making wine for personal consumption. Besides serving wine as a typical part of an Italian meal, during the summer, Elsie served lunch and dinner on their screened-in porch to the grape-pickers working in the vineyards. To retrieve cool pitchers of wine to serve with their meal, Elsie simply lifted the trap door next to the table on the porch to gain access to the wine cellar.

But not all the bottles of wine Joe produced could be considered 'for personal consumption.' He also supplied wine and other types of liquor to outsiders. Using the secret tunnels to access the property around the still, Joe hid bottles in the rock wall and cactus which his customers retrieved from their hiding places. When Mt. Gleason Junior High was constructed, tractors kept sinking into the old tunnels. The builders finally contacted Tony to pinpoint the location of the tunnels so they could avoid further accidents.

As a Mafia boss, Joe tried to 'muscle in' on other bootlegging and smuggling businesses. A gang war started during an argument between Joe and two bootleggers from 'Little Italy' in Los Angeles. In February, 1931, Joe invited

Jimmy Basile, one of those bootleggers, for a 'ride.' Basile's friends saw Jimmy in Downey with Joe and opened fire on the car. Joe crawled away, wounded but alive. Jimmy did not fare as well—he was caught in the crossfire. While Joe battled with local rivals, he also quarreled with Eastern interests trying to 'muscle in' on him.

Joe disrupted the status quo of the Mafia and made enemies. While he recuperated at Hollywood Presbyterian Hospital, his brothers and nephews took turns as armed guards and foiled a second attempt on his life. As an extra precaution, Joe wouldn't eat the hospital food; a personal cook brought his lunch and dinner.

His youngest sister, Christina, nicknamed Tini because of her diminutive four-foot-eleven inches and size-four shoe, constantly worried and warned Joe. "They're after you," she'd say, or "Don't go by yourself." Although he carried a Colt revolver in the car on the seat next to him, Joe seemed more concerned with his family's safety than his own.

One day after stopping at the library, Tony and Josephine arrived home later than usual. Elsie loved to read to the children and passed on her love for books. They enjoyed such classics as *Heidi, Little Women, Anne of Green Gables, Nancy Drew mysteries, Tom Swift,* and *Tarzan*. With their mother's permission, they stopped at the one-room library near Fenwick and Floralita after school to return and borrow books. This day, however, their father came home from work very early. Furious, fearful for their safety, he lashed at them verbally, insisting they never go alone again, but just come straight home from school. Too bad Joe didn't listen to his own advice.

In that simpler time, parents didn't have to teach kids lessons like "Don't take rides from strangers." But Tony and Josephine did not live the ordinary life of other Sunland kids. Perhaps her father's fear had communicated itself in more ways than just words. One day a stranger stopped Josephine as she was walking home. Scared, she ran the rest of the way, realizing her father would have killed the man if he had witnessed the incident. And she was quite literally correct. The "Iron Man" supposedly admitted to killing 30 unwilling business associates as he threatened the 31st.[6]

On October 15, 1931[7], Joe left home at 6:30 a.m. for a short trip to a ranch near Ettiwanda to pick up a relative. Hopefully, he kissed his wife and children fondly in parting, for they would never see him again. The man and his automobile simply disappeared into history. For weeks, the police searched for clues, but to no avail. At the time, Elsie was 33, Tony 14, and Josephine 11. Joe was officially declared dead seven years later.

The Ardizzones -- Joe, Tony, Elsie, and Josephine -- at their home on Mt. Gleason Avenue. Photo courtesy of the Ardizone family.

Life after Joe

Elsie's life changed once more. No more fine clothes or lavish jewels. No more large parties, elegant dinners, or oceanside vacations. No more 'friends' from other Mafia families who immediately severed all ties with her. She'd lost her husband and her security, but not her pioneer spirit.

Joe's disappearance during the Great Depression compounded Elsie's predicament. The cigar box of promissory notes from people who owed Joe thousands and thousands of dollars proved to be valueless when they failed to repay the loans. Whether they couldn't or wouldn't is irrelevant; the fact is, they didn't. When so many people lived on the edge of starvation, few had the resources to reach out to Elsie and her children. Only her sister Frances and her brother-in-law Cecil came faithfully once a week with groceries or clothes for the kids.

Without help, except for their faithful foreman, Sponnie, who stayed on without pay, Elsie survived on her own ingenuity. She fought to keep the ranch by marketing homemade wine, and selling off furniture, winery equipment, and rooms full of tools. Because of the Depression, they sold for a fraction of their value. She rented the extra house, formerly for workers, for income. In spite of her efforts, she lost the battle with the mortgage two years later and moved to 10610 Pinyon Street in Tujunga, while Josephine attended high school in San Fernando. Later, she moved again to 10407 Eldora Street in Sunland.

Just before he disappeared, Joe had given Tony a new Ford Cabriolet convertible. Joe surprised his kids by picking them up from school on Tony's birthday. As they turned into the driveway lined with lots of friends and relatives, a band started playing. There in the driveway, decorated with ribbons, waited Tony's present. At the time, the Ardizzones had four other cars: a Lincoln, two Fords, and a truck. Elsie sold these, and when they moved to Pinyon Street, aside from being a fond memory of Joe, Tony's car provided their sole means of transportation.

Never embittered by her tragic loss, Elsie remained sociable and friendly, her home open to her friends and those of her children. The kids hosted many a party; they'd roll up the rug in the big living room and dance to the music from their record player—one of the last gifts from their father. When a new family moved into the neighborhood several houses down, Elsie insisted

Josephine go welcome the daughter and bring the girl back to join the fun.

Elsie worked at the Wooden Rattler Restaurant on the corner of Mt. Gleason and Foothill. Joe originally constructed the building in 1929 as a fruit stand. When that didn't work, it became a soda fountain, an ice house, and finally a restaurant. Fortunately, Elsie retained title to the property when the bank foreclosed on the ranch. Elsie and her boyfriend Patty McMann took over the restaurant which gained popularity with Elsie's famous French dip sandwiches and hamburgers, and they added a beer and wine bar.

Tony's Café has changed hands several times over the years.

After years of staying at home, Elsie loved her new role. "When she got out and went to work at that bar, it was just like a new life for her. She met a lot of people, and they all loved her. She'd rather be there than anywhere else."[8]

Advertisement in The Record-Ledger 7/28/55

The Old Timers Celebration was an annual event of spoof and fun commemorating Sunland's origin.

In the late 1940s, her son Tony took over the restaurant and renamed it Tony's Café. Until 1967, Elsie remained as the official manager, cooking and ordering supplies for her son. As the city widened Foothill Boulevard and Mt. Gleason Avenue, it sliced off pieces of the property until the sidewalks crept right up to the sides of the building. In the 1970s, Tony's Café sold. It has changed ownership several times since, functioning as a cocktail lounge.

Socially, Elsie remained very active. She participated in the Foothill Funsters, enjoyed trips to Las Vegas, the horse races, and an occasional toddy. At home she enjoyed playing the piano and raising African violets. Personally she remained very disciplined, running her life on a schedule, and always dressed stylishly, complete with scarf and gloves.

Elsie Elizabeth Ellenberg Ardizzone died on March 5, 1987, at the age of 89. With her died an unusual chapter in the history of Sunland.

#####

Footnotes

[1] This was probably part of the land brought by Hartranft in 1907 and subdivided into plots of 5, 10, and 20 acres.
[2] Joe's son Tony later changed the spelling of the family name to Ardizone, with one z. Early records use two z's so that is the spelling used when appropriate.
[3] *The Grim Reapers*, pp. 3-4.
[4] Jack Dragna's real name was Anthony Rizzoti. He came from Corleone, Sicily, in 1908.
[5] McGroarty's home became the McGroarty Arts Center, 7570 McGroarty Terrace, Tujunga.
[6] *The Grim Reapers*, p. 165.
[7] Joe's disappearance coincided with Al Capone's trial for tax evasion. Capone was convicted two days after Joe disappeared on October 17, 1931.
[8] Personal interview with Josephine Kemp by Mary Lee Tiernan. July 19, 1999.

Bibliography

"Ardizzone Case Report Denied." *The Los Angeles Times*, October 20, 1931.

Ardizone, Caroline. Personal interview by Mary Lou Pozzo. November 1, 1997.

Ardizone, Caroline. Personal interview by Mary Lou Pozzo. April 25, 1998.

"Bootleg Gangs Open New War." *The Los Angeles Times*, October 18, 1931.

"Fire Destroys House Owned by Joe Ardizzone." *The Record-Ledger*, Thursday, March 19, 1924.

Hartranft, Edward. Personal Interview. March 30, 1974.

Kemp, Josephine (Ardizone). Personal interview by Mary Lee Tiernan. July 19, 1999.

Reid, Ed. *The Grim Reapers: The Anatomy of Organized Crime in America.* Chicago: Henry Regnery Company, 1969.

"Salvatore Ardizzone, Early Valley Settler, Farmer, Dies at Age 79." *The Record-Ledger*, Thursday, March 27, 1958.

"Search Futile for Ardizzone." *The Los Angeles Times*, October 21, 1931.

"Winery Found in Haystacks." *The Los Angeles Times*, October 24, 1931.

The Early History of Sunland, California

8 Volume Series
Also available as ebooks

Vol. 1 *Hotels for the Hopeful* Land promoters of the 1880s promised a perfect life of health, wealth, and pleasure. Although their promises fell short of reality, the village did grow and prosper in the hands of farmers.

Vol. 2 *The Roscoe Robbers and the Sensational Train Robbery of 1894* Two robbers posed as passengers to flag down the train. When the engineer recognized danger, he opened the throttle and sped past. The bandits threw the spur switch, and the train careened full speed off the tracks.

Vol. 3 *The Parson and His Cemetery* Parson Wornum was so loved that when he died, the whole village attended his funeral. Years of neglect of his cemetery spelled disaster in 1978 when heavy rains tore open graves and washed bodies down the hillside.

Vol. 4 *From Crackers to Coal Oil*   When a student pulled out his gun and laid it on his desk, the tiny one-room school found itself needing a new teacher. That brought Virginia Newcomb, a romance, and a new family that helped to develop the town, leaving behind a detailed account of pioneer life in a small village.

Vol. 5 *He Never Came Home*   Joe Ardizzone, a local grape-grower, doubled as a hit-man for the Mafia. During Prohibition, Joe's bootlegging activities caught him in the middle of in-house quarreling. In 1931, he left on a short trip and disappeared into the pages of history.

Vol. 6 *Lancasters Lake*   When Edgar Lancaster dredged the swamp on his land, he created a lake which became a treasured landmark. For 25 years, visitors flocked to its cool shores, and Hollywood used the lake as a set location for some of its early movies.

Vol. 7 *Living in Big Tujunga Canyon*   Early settlers, like the Johnson family, found their way into the canyon, a dense woodland bristling with wildlife. 50 years later, the Webber family faced the wrath of the river now winding down a denuded mountainside.

Vol. 8 *From Whence They Came* The Land Boom of the 1880s brought immigrants from around the world. Two generations of Blumfields survived the difficulties of farming and water shortages through industry and imagination.

www.ingramcontent.com/pod-product-compliance
Lightning Source LLC
Chambersburg PA
CBHW061348040426
42444CB00011B/3150